INVASIVE SPECIES

EMERALD ASH BORERS

by Alicia Z. Klepeis

pogo

Ideas for Parents and Teachers

Pogo Books let children practice reading informational text while introducing them to nonfiction features such as headings, labels, sidebars, maps, and diagrams, as well as a table of contents, glossary, and index.

Carefully leveled text with a strong photo match offers early fluent readers the support they need to succeed.

Before Reading

- "Walk" through the book and point out the various nonfiction features. Ask the student what purpose each feature serves.
- Look at the glossary together. Read and discuss the words.

Read the Book

- Have the child read the book independently.
- Invite him or her to list questions that arise from reading.

After Reading

- Discuss the child's questions. Talk about how he or she might find answers to those questions.
- Prompt the child to think more. Ask: Emerald ash borers spend their entire lives in and around ash trees. Can you name other insects or animals that use trees for shelter?

Pogo Books are published by Jump!
5357 Penn Avenue South
Minneapolis, MN 55419
www.jumplibrary.com

Library of Congress Cataloging-in-Publication Data

Names: Klepeis, Alicia, 1971- author.
Title: Emerald ash borers / by Alicia Z. Klepeis.
Description: Minneapolis, MN: Jump!, Inc., [2023]
Series: Invasive species | Includes index.
Audience: Ages 7-10
Identifiers: LCCN 2021062537 (print)
LCCN 2021062538 (ebook)
ISBN 9781636907925 (hardcover)
ISBN 9781636907932 (paperback)
ISBN 9781636907949 (ebook)
Subjects: LCSH: Emerald ash borer—Juvenile literature.
Introduced insects—Juvenile literature.
Classification: LCC QL596.B8 K54 2023 (print) | LCC QL596.B8 (ebook) | DDC 595.76/3—dc23/eng/20211223
LC record available at https://lccn.loc.gov/2021062537
LC ebook record available at https://lccn.loc.gov/2021062538

Editor: Eliza Leahy
Designer: Michelle Sonnek

Photo Credits: Monique van Someren/Shutterstock, cover, 6-7, 23; Monique van Someren/Getty, 1; Macroscopic Solutions/Science Source, 3; Wolfgang Hoffmann/Design Pics/Getty, 4; EuVigil/Shutterstock, 5; toondelamour/iStock, 8; Robert Winkler/iStock, 9; catnap72/iStock, 10-11, 14-15; Zadiraka Evgenii/Shutterstock, 12-13 (top); Science History Images/Alamy, 12-13 (bottom); K Steve Cope/Shutterstock, 16-17; Photawa/iStock, 18; Robert Nickelsberg/Getty, 19; Ozgur Coskun/Shutterstock, 20-21.

Printed in the United States of America at Corporate Graphics in North Mankato, Minnesota.

TABLE OF CONTENTS

CHAPTER 1

TINY AND SHINY

What insects are less than one inch (2.5 centimeters) long but can kill big trees? They are emerald ash borers. These beetles bore, or dig, under the bark of ash trees. This can kill the trees.

These beetles are long and thin. They are shiny. From above, they look green. They each have two **antennas**. These help them smell. The beetles' eyes are big and black.

abdomen
inner wing
outer wing

Each beetle has two pairs of wings. The outer pair is hard. They protect the soft inner pair. The inner wings are used for flying. When an emerald ash borer lifts its wings, you can see its red **abdomen**.

CHAPTER 2

WATCH OUT, TREES!

Emerald ash borers are native to parts of Asia. In North America, they are an invasive species.

People first saw them in the United States in 2002. How did they get here? Scientists are not sure. They may have come in ash wood on a ship or plane from Asia.

The **climate** in North America is similar to where the beetles live in Asia. They easily eat ash trees here. This is not the case in Asia. Why? The wood of Asian ash trees is not as easy to eat. This keeps the number of beetles there small.

TAKE A LOOK!

Emerald ash borers have spread across much of the United States and Canada. Take a look!

In Asia, woodpeckers eat emerald ash borers. Wasps attack the beetles' eggs and **larvae**. But emerald ash borers don't have many **predators** in North America. They **reproduce** more. They kill more trees.

DID YOU KNOW?

Emerald ash borers have killed tens of millions of ash trees in Michigan.

woodpecker

wasp

tunnel

Emerald ash borers reproduce their entire adult lives. Females lay eggs in ash tree bark. Larvae hatch. They chew through the bark. Then they make tunnels inside the tree. They eat the tree's **tissue**. The larvae grow there for several months.

In spring, the beetles are adults. They chew out of the tree. They fly away. Females lay eggs in another ash tree. The **cycle** starts over.

The tunnels larvae make eventually kill the tree. How? They stop water and **nutrients** from reaching all parts of the tree.

The top of an **infested** tree usually dies first. The leaves thin out. Then, the branches die. A large tree may die within three or four years. A smaller tree can die within a year or two.

DID YOU KNOW?

In infested trees, new branches sometimes grow from the bottom of the trunk. Why? The tree is trying to grow wherever it can.

infested
ash tree

CHAPTER 3

BATTLING THE BEETLES

Many people are working to stop the spread of emerald ash borers. How? They put out traps. The beetles get stuck. They die.

Arborists use **pesticides**. They **inject** them into ash trees. If the beetles eat the wood, they die.

maple tree

Scientists release wasps. These wasps come from Asia, too. They attack the beetles' larvae and eggs.

We can all help stop the spread of invasive species. Learn about insects that live near you. Plant native trees. The wildlife will thank you!

DID YOU KNOW?

Emerald ash borers can live in firewood. What happens if it is moved? The beetles move with it. Only buy local firewood. This keeps the beetles from spreading to new areas.

ACTIVITIES & TOOLS

TRY THIS!

BEETLES NEAR YOU

North American ash trees are in danger because of emerald ash borers. Learn about the beetles in your area in this fun activity!

What You Need:

- a computer, books, or magazines
- sheets of paper
- colored pencils, crayons, or markers
- tape or glue
- a large sheet of paper or posterboard

1. **Use a computer, books, or magazines to find out what beetles are native to your area. Pick two.**
2. **Learn what the beetles look like and how large they get.**
3. **Draw one of the beetles on a piece of paper. Record its size.**
4. **Repeat Step 3 for the other beetle.**
5. **Tape or glue your drawings to your large paper or posterboard.**
6. **What are some similarities between the native beetles you researched and emerald ash borers? What are some differences?**

GLOSSARY

abdomen: The rear section of an insect's body.

antennas: Feelers on the heads of insects.

arborists: People who work to take care of trees and make sure trees are healthy.

climate: The weather typical of a certain place over a long period of time.

cycle: A series of events that repeats in the same order.

infested: Having insects present in large numbers, which can cause damage or disease.

inject: To force a liquid into something.

invasive species: Any kind of living organism that is not native to a specific area.

larvae: Insects in the stage of development between eggs and pupae.

native: Growing or living naturally in a particular area of the world.

nutrients: Substances such as proteins, minerals, and vitamins that people, animals, and plants need to stay strong and healthy.

pesticides: Chemicals used to kill pests, such as insects.

predators: Animals that hunt other animals for food.

reproduce: To produce offspring.

tissue: The material that forms the parts of a plant or animal.

INDEX

TO LEARN MORE

Finding more information is as easy as 1, 2, 3.

1. Go to www.factsurfer.com
2. Enter "emeraldashborers" into the search box.
3. Choose your book to see a list of websites.

FACT SURFER